TEACHING STRATEGIES
for ACTIVE
LEARNING

This book is dedicated to my parents, Jack and Jacqueline Walker, who have always believed that their children can accomplish anything.

Donna Walker Tileston

TEACHING STRATEGIES
for ACTIVE
LEARNING

Five Essentials for Your Teaching Plan

CORWIN PRESS
A SAGE Publications Company
Thousand Oaks, CA 91320

For information:

Corwin Press
A Sage Publications Company
2455 Teller Road
Thousand Oaks, California 91320
www.corwinpress.com

Sage Publications Ltd.
1 Oliver's Yard
55 City Road
London EC1Y 1SP
United Kingdom

Sage Publications India Pvt. Ltd.
B-42, Panchsheel Enclave
Post Box 4109
New Delhi 110 017 India

Printed in the United States of America

Library of Congress Cataloging-in-Publication Data

Tileston, Donna Walker.
Teaching strategies for active learning : five essentials for your teaching plan / Donna Walker Tileston.
    p. cm.
Includes bibliographical references and index.
ISBN 0-7619-3854-0 or 978-0-7619-3854-5 (cloth)
ISBN 0-7619-3855-9 or 978-0-7619-3855-2 (pbk.)
    1. Active learning. 2. Effective teaching. I. Title.

LB1027.23.T55 2007
371.102—dc22

2006025712

This book is printed on acid-free paper.

06 07 08 09 10   10 9 8 7 6 5 4 3 2 1

Acquisitions Editor:	Faye Zucker
Editorial Assistant:	Gem Rabanera
Production Editor:	Catherine M. Chilton
Copy Editor:	Marilyn Power Scott
Typesetter:	C&M Digitals (P) Ltd.
Proofreader:	Doris Hus
Indexer:	Jeanne R. Busemeyer
Cover Designer:	Scott Van Atta
Graphic Designer:	Audrey Snodgrass

Contents

Preface

Learning is a very different process than attention.

—Eric Jensen (1997, p. 27)

This book is written to incorporate what we know about how the brain learns and remembers—the order of the processes that seem to bring about the highest effects on student learning. It does not matter where we begin teaching our lessons; our students' brains begin in the self-system. If we want to tap into the natural incentives to learn, we must begin where our students are, and that involves the self-system. There is an order to learning that seems (through meta-analysis studies) to provide a greater response by the brain to the new information. How we teach is just as important as what we teach in terms of storage and retrieval. Within this book, you will be guided through a step-by-step process for powerful lessons that make a difference in student learning because they are based on the latest information on the brain.

The uniqueness of this model is that it is systemic rather than piecemeal. One of the reasons that models so often fail to live up to their promises is that they have either addressed only a single experience in one school or only a small portion of the process. You can find books that address motivation or assessment or metacognition. This book addresses all of the key aspects of the learning process. While the pilot school for these strategies showed remarkable results, the meta-analysis of many, many studies is also provided to back up the research. We live in an age of accountability, and it is important to ask of any research the following two questions:

- What does the meta-analysis of many studies say about the expected results of using this strategy?

Tileston (2006) explains meta-analysis as a study of the studies relating to given techniques and the effects of those techniques on actual student learning when compared to the learning of students who were not exposed to the techniques. Figure P.1 provides an example: Suppose that a classroom average for understanding vocabulary is at the 50th percentile. If we employ a certain method for teaching vocabulary, what does meta-analysis say will be the effect on student learning? In

Figure P.1   Meta-Analysis Example

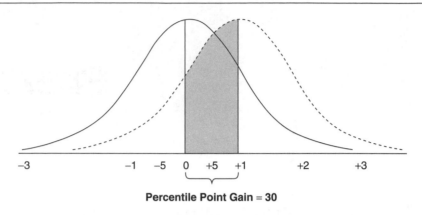

Percentile Point Gain = 30

this case, the effect was .84, meaning that the average effect size for the students in the experimental group was .84 standard deviation higher than those of the control group.

One of the useful features of using meta-analysis is that these scores can be interpreted into percentile points. An overall effect size of .84 translates into 30 percentile points. In other words, students exposed to the given method for teaching vocabulary have shown an increase in their learning by 30 percentile points over those in a control group that did not receive the same instructional practice. This research is key to making good choices about which instructional strategy to use in the classroom. In this book, where appropriate, you will be given the average effect sizes and percentile point gains for the various strategies.

- Under what conditions does the strategy work best?

While many books on the market today would have you believe that whatever strategy they are pitching works across the board, there are only a handful of strategies that do. Most strategies work differently depending on whether you are teaching declarative or procedural information and in what system of the brain you are working. For example, when introducing a unit of study, you are usually tapping into the self-system of the brain that constitutes the feelings, emotions and motivations of the learner. Strategies that have been shown through meta-analysis to have a high effect on learning at that stage of the lesson may be very different from the strategies that might be employed while teaching a process in the cognitive system.

DOES THE STRATEGY FOLLOW CURRENT BRAIN RESEARCH?

Most of the books on the market address interesting activities to be used in the classroom but lack a systemic plan for using them. Thus teachers are left with disjointed activities that they must try to fit into the lessons. These chapters are about a different approach to teaching and learning.

This book represents years of research on the factors that encourage learning and those that impede learning, whether the class is 45 minutes in length or lasts for several hours. In a classroom where quality learning is taking place, a set of characteristics is present. I call this set of characteristics *strategic learning* because it follows a specific plan (strategy) and has as its goal quality learning that leads to long-term memory retention. In a strategic-learning classroom, students are taught in an environment conducive to maximum learning. They are taught meaningful, relevant information that connects to their world and the world in which they will live as adults. Although lecture has its place in some lessons, it should only be used in short segments of time—15 minutes or less in secondary classrooms and 5–10 minutes in elementary school, based on the age of the children. It is unrealistic to believe that students who are constantly stimulated by the multimedia world will sit for hours each day passively listening to lectures, taking notes, and preparing for the pencil-and-paper exam on Friday—all this without dropping out mentally. Life is not a spectator sport; it is an exercise in active involvement: Education should reflect that active involvement.

For 6 years, I was involved in a dynamic research project that examined the factors that enhance learning and why they did so. The results of that study are dramatic and touch at the heart of how schools should teach. The project school was transformed into a place of strategic learning. Within 2 years, the results were impressive The dropout rate went from 7.4% before implementation to 2.2% at the 2-year mark—and today shows a dropout rate of 0%. Attendance rates increased by almost 4%. Scholastic Aptitude Test scores zoomed to well above state and national averages, and what is more, students and teachers wanted to go to school each day. In a statistical study of the students over time, it was found that reading and mathematics scores for both males and females rose significantly. All of this was accomplished in a school district where more than 50% of the population qualified for free or reduced-cost lunches under the national poverty standards.

I have applied the meta-analysis studies on instructional practices to my research with some phenomenal results. Thanks to this incredible body of knowledge, we no longer have to guess which practices will have the highest effect on student learning—we know. While many books on the market will provide blanket strategies for the classroom, we now know that there are no blanket strategies, but rather, strategies are effective depending on the area of the brain engaged at the time of instruction. For example, cooperative–collaborative learning has a high effect size when students are practicing a particular learning or when the goal is to create a positive learning climate, but the effect size is low when this strategy is used to introduce a topic.

This book is divided into five chapters. Chapter 1 talks about how and why we must move from the structures of the past to a new way of teaching that better prepares students in the 21st century. It also introduces a format for active learning that I call the *Strategic Learning Model*. This model follows current research on how the brain learns and remembers best.

Chapters 2 and 3 relate to the self-system of the brain. This system is sometimes called the *gatekeeper to motivation*. In Chapter 2, I introduce the first phase of the Strategic-Learning Model, called Plugging In. This chapter is about those strategies that help us to create the kind of learning environment that is "brain friendly." Eric Jensen (1997) talks about this kind of environment in terms of the neural systems that run our lives. This includes strategies that tap into the cerebral cortex's need for newness, novelty, and high contrast. It includes the midbrain's need for things that provide pleasure and positive feelings and the lower brain's desire for an environment that is safe—both physically and emotionally.

Chapter 3 introduces the second phase of the learning model, called Powering Up. This chapter focuses on strategies that tap into our natural motivation to learn. Our brains seem to be hardwired to learn—it is one of the reasons that we have survived as a species. Environmental effects tamper with that natural motivation, and as teachers, we must utilize strategies that rekindle that desire to learn. These first three chapters are so important that without them, the information from the other chapters is powerless.

Chapter 4 deals with the components needed to deliver differentiated instruction to students. I call this process *synthesis* because our students are taking a great deal of incoming information from the senses and synthesizing it into meaningful information to help them, not just for the moment but for life. Chapter 5 discusses how to ensure that students understand the information studied by requiring that they demonstrate the learning in some way. I call this *outsourcing* because they are taking the information that they learned in the synthesis phase and outsourcing it to meaningful processes. The last section, Chapter 6, provides the real-world connection to the learning. The goal is not only to help students learn but to help them put the information into long-term memory. One of the ways that we can help the brain to do this is to provide opportunities for reflection. The time when the information in this book will have the most meaning to you is when you have an opportunity to think about it, to apply it to your world and to talk about it to yourself and others.

This is a very different type of classroom from the one most often found in schools, where teachers are the imparters of knowledge in a lecture format while students memorize facts to give back on pencil-and-paper tests. The transformation takes time and commitment, but it is worth it because it is better for kids.

Acknowledgments

I want to thank the awesome staff at Corwin Press who continually believe in my work and help to make my words useful and accessible to educators: Robb Clouse who watches over it all, Gem Rabanera who works so hard to edit my work and, of course, my friend and master editor at Corwin Press, Faye Zucker.

Corwin Press thanks the following reviewers for their contributions to this book:

Russ Adams, Principal, MOC-Floyd Valley High, Orange City, IA

Patricia Bowman, Principal, C. Morley Sellery School, Gardena, CA

Kevin Brandon, Teacher, John Burroughs Middle School, Los Angeles, CA

Richard Cash, Director of Gifted Education, Bloomington Public Schools, Bloomington, MN

Beverly Eidmann, Principal, Arvada Middle School, Arvada, CO

Christine Goldberg, NBCT, Phoenix High School, Dalton, GA

Cindy Harrison, Educational Consultant, Thornton, CO

Toby Karten, Graduate Instructor, College of New Jersey and Gratz College, PA

About the Author

 **Donna Walker Tileston**, EdD, has served education as a leader in teaching, administration, research, writing, software development, and national consulting for the past 30 years. Her administrative responsibilities have included curriculum development, management, technology, finance, grants management, public relations, and drug abuse prevention programs. For the past 25 years Tileston has been actively involved in brain research and the factors that inhibit learning or increase the brain's ability to put information into long-term memory.

Dr. Tileston's research has been published through Corwin Press under the titles *Strategies for Teaching Differently* (1998), *Ten Best Teaching Practices: How Brain Research, Learning Styles and Standards Define Teaching Competencies* (2000, 2005), *What Every Parent Should Know About Schools, Standards, and High-Stakes Tests* (2005), and *What Every Teacher Should Know: The Ten-Book Collection* (2003). This last received the 2004 Distinguished Achievement Award for Excellence in Educational Publishing by the American Educational Publishers Association.

To date, Dr. Tileston has made over 400 presentations on her research at local, state, national and international conferences, most recently at The Hague in November 2005 and in Prague in March 2006. Dr. Tileston can be reached at her office at 817-874-1258 or online at http://www.wetsk.com.

1

Teaching in the 21st Century

The world we have created is a product of our thinking; it cannot be changed without changing our thinking.

—Albert Einstein

We must prepare students for the world of their future—not the world of our past.

—Anonymous

Visit any bookstore today and you will be inundated by authors who are making predictions about what will be required of workers in this century. Much of what they say is already happening. Thomas Friedman's (2005) book, *The World is Flat*, gives us an alarming picture of a universal world in which any job that can be done cheaper or with more efficiency than in the United States will be outsourced—indeed is being outsourced as you read this book. The implications for our students are dramatic. They must be able to know both how to do something and how to do it in a way that cannot be easily duplicated. Just having facts will not be enough; in the future, students must be able to employ those more right-brain functions, such as synthesis, creativity, and esthetics.

Bill Gates has a question that he sometimes uses when talking about globalization and competition in this century. He asks his audience whether 20 years ago, they would rather have been a "B" student in Poughkeepsie or a genius in Shanghai. Then he asks them about their feelings on this today (quoted in the Benton, 2005). Anyone traveling to Shanghai today will find that the genius there is being utilized to the fullest extent with new skyscrapers, new technology, and new jobs.

Figure 1.1   The Strategic Learning Model

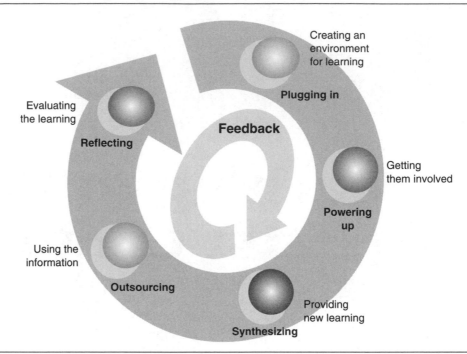

Daniel Pink (2005), in his cutting-edge new book, *A Whole New Mind*, poses three questions that we should be asking ourselves as we model the curriculum, the lessons, the standards and, yes, even those high-stakes tests:

1. Can someone overseas do it cheaper?
2. Can a computer do it faster?
3. Am I offering something that satisfies the nonmaterial transcendent desires of an abundant age? (p. 232)

These questions will guide the job market for the students that we have in our classrooms right now. What we teach and how we teach it will have a profound effect on whether our students fit into the new literacy for the job market in this century.

Who are these kids sitting in the classroom? They are certainly different from generations past—not just in the way they dress, the piercing, the fidgeting, the off-task behavior, but also in the ways that they learn and communicate. Students today are comfortable with multitasking. In fact, they can send text messages while watching a movie and talking on the phone, all at the same time, without missing a beat. They are easily bored, and they just don't learn like the students of the past. What is a teacher to do? What do we know now that we didn't know then? Let's start with some things that we know about today's learners.

1. *They are wired differently.* We come into this world with about 50% of our wiring in place; the other 50% comes about as a result of our environment. Our parents and grandparents grew up in a time in which listening was the primary modality for learning. They listened to the radio, listened to each other as they sat around the dinner table at night, and they listened to the teacher as he or she lectured. They could do that effectively because their brains had been wired to listen

from a very young age. Students today really are neurologically wired differently. From a young age they have been actively using technology, multitasking and generally bombarded by a multimedia world. The wiring of the brain has been developed to follow that pattern. They do not learn by sitting and listening to a lecture alone, and they may not get excited when the teacher asks them to memorize the capitals of all the states. The student may be thinking, "Why should I memorize the capitals—if I want to know the capital of a state, I'll Google it."

2. *The primary mode of learning is visual or visual–kinesthetic.* More than 80% of the students in any given classroom are not auditory learners, yet the prevailing method of teaching—particularly in secondary schools—centers on lecture. Students today need to see the learning, and they need to interact with it.

3. *Being average is not enough.* That may have worked in a different economy where the assumption was that 20% of the students would do well, at least 20% would fail and the rest would be "C" students. The job market had plenty of work for the "average student." While America still enjoys some of the same economic advantages of the past—namely, a free market, access to capital, and a climate that accepts entrepreneurship—other parts of the world are gaining on us. Being a "C" student is a scary perspective in this day and time. We must change the way that we teach so that we teach to the modalities of all of our students, and we must realize that the digital learners of today need to do more than hear the learning—they need to see it and do something with it. As Daniel Pink (2005) says, the markets of the future demand that we don't just accumulate a lot of information but that we have the ability to detect the importance of the information, know how to synthesize it and put it in a format easily understood by the masses.

What, then, are the principal strategies of a strategic classroom and of a model built around this kind of classroom? Here are some of the basic characteristics that will be discussed throughout this book:

1. *There is a high level of support for achievement.* Teachers and students not only expect quality work, they will not accept anything less.

2. *Students are given a rubric up front*, before an assignment is made, so that they know what is expected. There is no "gotcha" attitude. Students know what they must do to be successful, and they are given the tools to help make success possible. We usually think of learning in terms of the normal bell curve, where a small number are toward the high end of achievement and a small number are at the low end, with the majority in the middle, or average. The bell curve assumes that some will fail and some will excel, but most will be mediocre. That has never been acceptable to me. If students are coming to school and are doing their best and there is still a bell curve, something is wrong with the system. The bell curve should occur before intervention, not after. If teaching follows the principles of strategic learning, there will be a j-curve: There will be a small number at the bottom and a small number at the center, with the majority at the top. That is what happened in the pilot school. When all students began to learn at a quality level, the overall failure rate dropped to below 4%—a j-curve.

3. *Higher-order thinking is emphasized for everyone.* Students are given meaningful, challenging work. It is an insult to give students mounds of dittos to complete to fill up time. Time on task is important only if the task is meaningful.

4. *There is an emphasis on depth of learning* rather than just covering a great deal of material. Students are given sufficient time and resources to make the learning a part of long-term memory.

5. *Connections are made to the real world and between the learnings.* Most students can be taught anything as long as it is relevant to their world. Glasser (as cited in Gough, 1988) says that is why young children learn one of the most difficult things to learn and learn it without flash cards—they learn a language. One of my favorite math teachers has a sign in her room that should be in every classroom in the United States. It says, "I promise I will never teach you anything in this classroom unless I can tell you how you are going to use it in the real world."

6. *The classroom emphasizes collaboration and dialogue.* To be successful in the job market, students must be able to articulate what they know and listen to the ideas and opinions of others. Students practice cooperative learning strategies to help solidify what they have learned and to practice the learning so that when it is time for individual assessment, the learning is in long-term memory. Sizer (1992) says,

   The real world demands collaboration, the collective solving of problems. . . . Learning to get along, to function effectively in a group is essential. Evidence and experience also strongly suggest that an individual's personal learning is enhanced by collaborative effort. The act of sharing ideas, of having to put one's own views clearly to others, of finding defensible compromises and conclusions, is in itself educative. (p. 118)

7. *Assessment is a natural progression of the lesson*, not something that is tacked on at the end to provide grades for the grade book. Students are told up front, before the lesson begins, what they must do to demonstrate success. The lines between the goals of the lesson and the assessment are blurred.

8. *The environment in the classroom is collaborative and supportive.* Climate is so important that none of the other techniques discussed will be really effective unless the issue of climate is settled first. In a world full of broken relationships, strong, supportive relationships are important to students. We cannot control the students' environment outside of the classroom, but for 7 hours each day, we have a great deal of control over their environment. It may be our best chance to make the world a better place.

9. *Technology is a seamless tool that is a part of the day-to-day teaching and learning process.* Today's students have never known a world without technology. They have literally grown up digital; they speak digital as their native language. Those of us over 30 speak digital as a second language. We must learn to incorporate technology into our teaching repertoire and into our students' work. Technology should not be an add-on but an essential tool, just as a pencil was to our generation.

Teaching for long-term memory is critical. After years of research on the factors that help students learn and remember as well as the factors that prevent understanding and retention, a model for teaching has emerged that is called, appropriately, the Strategic Learning Model. It is called the *learning* model because the emphasis is on student learning—where it belongs. Figure 1.1 (p. 2) is a graphic representation of this model.

ELEMENTS OF THE STRATEGIC LEARNING MODEL

The first element is called Plugging In. When I am working with schools, I often ask teachers, "What is the single most important thing that is keeping you from having the classroom of your dreams?" The answer is almost unanimous: "lack of student motivation." As a teacher, what can you do at the beginning of a lesson to ensure that your students have the elements necessary for the brain's natural instinct toward motivation?

The second element to the Strategic Learning Model is called Powering Up. Thanks to the use of magnetic resonance imaging (MRI), we now know that the brain is a seeker of connections. When new information is given to students, chaos may take place in the brain until a connection or hook is made. Unfortunately, the connection is never made for some students, and years of frustration and failure follow. Personal connection is the part of the lesson that provides a hook for the new learning and taps into the prior knowledge of the students.

The third phase of the Strategic Learning Model is Synthesizing. Finding and using sources of information is key, and examples are given for ways to teach in a differentiated classroom. This is the part of the lesson in which students acquire new information. Emphasis is placed on depth of learning, not just covering the text. At this stage in the lesson, students are active participants in the learning. They are sharing information, and they are practicing the learning together.

In the fourth phase of the model, called Outsourcing, we discuss how students apply the information in ways that are meaningful. In this part of the lesson, students use the new information to deepen their understanding and to demonstrate comprehension in some way. Concrete models are emphasized because as many as 80% of the learners in the classroom are likely to be visual learners.

The last chapter deals with helping students to evaluate their own learning and to make real-world connections. I call this part of the model Reflecting on the Learning.

Why didn't I include teacher assessment as a separate piece? Because assessment is an ongoing process in this model. Part of the reason for it is the immediate feedback and the incremental challenge. Immediate feedback is essential to this www generation who play digital games for hours without boredom.

THE TEACHER'S ROLE

The teacher's role in the strategic-learning classroom is critical and is based on the following six precepts:

1. Expect that all students can and will achieve at a quality level.

2. Accept only quality work on all student products. Accepting mediocre work is an insult to students and adults alike. Don't mistakenly believe that we raise students' self-concept by giving them watered-down work so that they will be successful. The brain likes and relates to challenge.

3. Help students understand the meaning, and connect the learning to prior knowledge or the real world rather than relying on simple drills or exercises to memorize routine facts to pass a test.

4. Serve more as a coach, guide and facilitator for the students' efforts to learn the material, and ensure that students will be active participants in the learning. "The leader in this role senses when and when not to intercede in the process; she or he is front and center when need arises, but assumes a low profile when the situation seems to be progressing well on its own" (Bellanca & Fogarty, 1991, p. 198).

5. Provide a variety of assessments that help to give a broad picture of each student's ability and that is directly aligned with the curriculum.

6. Engage students in meaningful work, and incorporate real-world application into the learning.

The strategic-learning classroom is, above all, student centered and follows the challenge to make learning meaningful. This requires a change in the way we view teaching. Many still believe that it is not education but the children who must change. The paradox is that children will not change until we change the way we approach the institution that teaches them. Einstein was right: "We will only change the world when we change our thinking."

2

Plugging In

What a wonderful time to be a teacher! Never before have we had available to us the answers to unlock the mysteries of the mind or to change the world in the way that we have at this time.

—Tileston (2004, p. xi)

PART 1 OF THE MODEL: PLUGGING IN

Instead of asking "How can I motivate students?" a better question would be, "In what ways is the brain naturally motivated from within?"

—Eric Jensen (1997)

Approximately 98% of all new learning comes into the brain through the senses; the other 2% comes through a connection between what we already know and the incoming information. In elementary school, we do a good job of using hearing, seeing, tasting, and feeling (tactile). As students move up the grade levels, most of the senses fall by the wayside, leaving hearing and some seeing. We teach digital learners who are comfortable with a multimedia world. As a matter of fact, they prefer to learn in a nonlinear, visual, tactile environment. No wonder they are dropping out mentally.

I often begin my workshops by asking educators what is keeping them from being the kind of teacher they dream of being. The answer is pretty unanimous: "unmotivated students." What is it that turns on motivation in the brain, and how can we tap into it? Marzano (2001) talks about the gatekeeper to motivation being

Figure 2.1 Strategic Learning Model: Plugging In

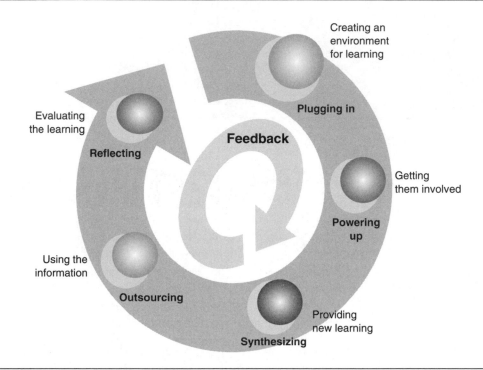

the self-system of the brain. The self-system is not a single place in the brain but the accumulation of various parts that are key to the brain's decision to pay attention. Research indicates that several factors work together to help us make the decision about whether we will pay attention or not. The following four factors seem to be paramount in that decision-making process:

1. *Personal relevance:* In business, sales people will tell you that a key factor in making a sale is to show the buyer what is in it for them personally, how it will help them to achieve a personal goal—whether it is money, prestige, acceptance, reaching a prescribed goal, or just making them feel better about themselves. The students ask, What does this learning have to do with my world? We can provide personal relevance to the learning by doing the following:

   a. Create a connection between the new learning and students' personal needs or goals. For example, we can stress that learning to estimate can help to keep them from being cheated. Learning about the environment can help them make better decisions about fuel when buying a car.

   b. Create a connection between the new learning and what students already know or have experienced. For example, before a unit on immigration, I ask students what would have to happen in this country to make them pick up whatever they could carry in their arms and go to live in a country where they knew no one. In elementary school, before reading the book *Henry Higgins* by Beverly Cleary, ask students what they would do if they found themselves in a situation much like the main character of this story who finds a lost dog, loves and cares for it, only to have the true owner show up to demand the dog back. Jensen (1997) says, "In order for information to be considered relevant, it must relate to something the learner already knows. It must activate a learner's existing neural networks. The more relevance, the greater the meaning" (p. 38).

   c. Ask students to write personal goals for the learning. For young elementary students, I might introduce the topic and ask them to tell me some things they would like to know. Go back often to the goals that are written or verbalized so that students can self-assess how well they are learning and achieving their goals. Model this behavior by posting your goals for the learning visually in the room and referring to them often.

2. *Meaning:* Learning without meaning is very difficult to move into the long-term memory system of the brain. We have all had the experience of memorizing something simply to pass a test—then forgetting it after the test. If we want our students to remember something forever, we need to be sure it has meaning for them. For students who are auditory learners, the opportunity to talk about the learning to themselves or others is important. Visual learners must "see" the learning before it has meaning, and for kinesthetic learners it is important to have the opportunity to interact with the learning.

3. *Positive self-efficacy:* We have heard much about the need for positive self-concepts. Self-esteem is how we feel about ourselves. It may or may not be based on fact; it is based on "I think and I feel." Self-efficacy is more powerful because it is built on the facts of past experiences. Self-esteem says, "I think I can be successful"; self-efficacy says, "I know I can be successful because I have been successful before." Self-efficacy is built when we have positive experiences with the learning, the subject, or individuals related to the learning. This is one of the reasons why success breeds success. Give students opportunities to be successful, even in incremental steps, so that they can build a sense of positive self-efficacy.

4. *Attitude:* How do students feel about the learning, the classroom, and the teacher? Students who go to a class each day with fear and dread will usually struggle in that classroom. To the extent possible make the classroom a place where students feel challenged but not threatened. You do not have to be their best friend, but they should feel comfortable asking questions, and they should believe it is OK not to know the answers—what is not OK is not to try. An important aspect of building a sense of community in the classroom is to use specific techniques to help students get to know one another and to build a sense of belonging among the group.

It does not matter where we begin our lessons; all learning begins in the self-system of the brain. Students come into our classrooms from the hall, from school buses, from home, with baggage. Maybe they had a disagreement with a family member before school or an encounter in the hallway, in a previous class or on the playground. They may be excited about an event that just took place or is about to take place. There may be anxiety about homework or the class that is about to begin. No wonder we have so much trouble making connections and creating momentum. Our students' brains begin in the self-system, which is considered to be the gatekeeper to motivation. We teachers, on the other hand, usually begin lessons in the cognitive system of the brain.

The self-system is not an actual spot in the brain but a combination of several parts of the brain that make up the emotions involved in deciding whether, in fact, to pay attention to new information. I have bad news and good news about the self-system. The bad news is that you cannot motivate your students—they are the only ones who can motivate themselves. The good news is that you can help to create the situations that lead to self-motivation in the brain.

SELF-EFFICACY AS A KEY TO MOTIVATION FOR LEARNING

Much has been said in the past generation about self-esteem and its importance to helping students to be successful. While self-esteem is important, self-efficacy may be more important to tapping into motivation. Many researchers today believe that self-efficacy is more important to motivation than self-esteem, especially as we work with students from poverty and students who have not had much success in the past. Thus it is important that students have positive experiences with the learning. That does not mean that we water down the learning but that we start with students where they are and give them opportunities to experience incremental successes.

The four attributes that affect the brain's decision to pay attention are not equally weighted. A student may not understand why the study of *slope* in mathematics is important personally but if the student likes the class and feels that success is possible, the student will more likely hang in there to see how the teacher is going to give it personal relevance.

ACTIVITIES FOR BUILDING A SENSE OF COMMUNITY IN THE CLASSROOM

At the beginning of the semester, take time to complete exercises with classes that will help students to get to know each other. The time taken for these activities will be rewarded many times over throughout the semester. Require students to call each other by their first names. Following are four examples of activities to help build a sense of community:

- Name That Name
- Question-and-Answer Profiles
- A Funny Thing Happened on My Way to. . . .
- Find Someone Who

Name That Name

This is a nonthreatening technique for introducing students to each other at the beginning of the semester. Because we require everyone to be called by their first names or preferred names, this is a good way to help students remember each other. The three steps for this technique are these:

1. Students are grouped into pairs.

2. Students interview each other using the following format:
   - What is your first name?
   - How did you get your name?
   - Is there something unique about your name that will help me remember it?

3. Students introduce each other to the rest of the class.

Variation

Use nametags with information about the student written in each corner, such as favorite sport, music, hobby, class, and so on.

Hobby	Best class
[NAME]	
Music	Favorite sport

Question-and-Answer Profiles

The purpose of question-and-answer profiles is to help students identify with each other. Team spirit is developed as members find common traits and goals. There are three steps:

1. Students work in groups of two, three, or four.

2. Students share information about themselves with the group.

3. The information is charted to determine likes and differences.

Ask students to look for common interests. A sample chart is shown in Table 2.1.

Table 2.1   Question-and-Answer Profiles

Directions: In your study groups, answer the questions below for each individual. Discuss areas where you are alike and areas where you are different as individuals.

Questions	First Person	Second Person	Third Person
My favorite musical group is			
My favorite sport is			
In my spare time I			
My best subject is			
If I could live anywhere, it would be			

A Funny Thing Happened on My Way to. . . .

There are five steps for this exercise:

1. Students are placed into groups of three or four.

2. Each student briefly shares an experience that relates to the topic given by the teacher.

3. The students decide together which experience they will write or tell.

4. All students in the group retell or write about the experience as if it happened to them.

5. A group is called on, and one student tells the experience. The class must guess which student really had the experience.

Example:

Read the wonderful book about math anxiety called *Math Curse*, by Jon Scieszka and Lane Smith (1995) in class. Next, ask the question, "Have you ever had trouble learning something important?"

Students share experiences in groups of three or four.

Each group chooses one experience to be their group's experience to share with the class.

The teacher calls on one person from the group to tell the experience. Ask the class to guess who really had the experience.

Find Someone Who

This technique has several purposes. It is a great tool for helping students get to know each other, but it is also a meaningful way to learn important information. The three steps are these:

1. Students are given a list of questions.

2. Each student finds other students in the room who can answer each one of the questions. Students initial or write first names by their answers.

3. Students must get a different signature on each question.

Variation:

Use as a review after material has been studied. Instead of personal questions, use questions about the lesson. For example,

Find Someone Who

Knows how to find the area of a polygon _____ Length × Width–*Margaret*

One of the advantages of using this exercise is that once a student finds an answer from another student, he or she becomes an expert on that question and can sign someone else's paper. Those students who never seem to know the answers are elevated to experts. Table 2.2 shows an example used to help students get to know each other and to determine common interests.

Table 2.2   Find Someone Who

Directions: Ask a different person to sign for each of the following.

Find Someone Who	Sign Here	Person and Details
Likes the same sport as you		Mark (baseball)
Has a blue car		Marta (Chevy)
Has two brothers		Rob (ages 8 and 11)
Plans to go to college in another state		Chris
Had an unusual summer job		Jessie (ocean guide)
Plans to become a lawyer		Paul
Likes to work with computers		Jack
Has a birthday in December		Kevin (17th)
Has been to Disneyworld		Lupe
Has an unusual hobby		Dave (taxidermy)

Trivia Pairs

For this activity, each student is given only part of the information needed. They must find the other person or persons who have the additional information they need. These students make up the group that is to work together for the activity. For example, one student is given the answer to a math equation and two other students are given the parts that make up the equation. These students must find the other students who have the information they need. When the three pieces of information are put together, they form a study group.

Variations:

- Give out a sequence of events on separate slips of paper and have student form groups by putting the events together.

- Give out the name of a country, its climate, location, and products on separate slips of paper and have students form groups by country and its characteristics.

- Pass out titles of songs for students to hum until they find others in the room who are humming the same song.

- Write information or trivia on puzzle parts that must be matched to form the group. For example, *Tora, Tora, Tora* might be written on one puzzle part and *Pearl Harbor* on the other part.

- In various parts of the room, place signs that say *first child, middle child, only child,* and *last child,* and ask students to go the part of the room that describes their birth order. Place students in groups from the four groups.

There are many variations of this exercise. Instead of using personal information, the teacher might use characters from literature and ask students to go to the area of the room that holds a sign naming a character with which they most identify. The teacher might divide the room according to concepts being studied and have students go to the area in which they have the most questions.

Team Name

Study groups who work together over a period of time may give their groups team names. The team names should only be assigned after the team has worked together long enough to know each other. The team name should reflect something about the team. For example, a team might call itself The Number Crunchers because they are very good at putting numbers together in some way or at working problems. Once the group has arrived at a name, the name should be used when referring to the collective group or on papers turned in by the group so that you acknowledge the group's identity.

A variation of this technique is called Bumper Stickers. For this activity, the group comes up with a bumper sticker that reflects their team spirit. Again, the bumper stickers should be used in some way to solidify the identity of the group.

_____

_____

_____

_____

_____

_____

_____

_____

_____

_____

_____

Appointments

One of my favorite methods of putting students into temporary groups for an activity is called Appointments and very much reflects the way we work in the business world. This is a good technique when you want students to work with many different students for short periods of time, for example, to review techniques studied or for problem solving. The following three steps should be followed:

1. Give each student a picture of the face of a clock (see Figure 2.2).

2. Each student sets appointments with other students in the classroom. Students put their first name by the appointment time.

3. When the teacher calls out an appointment time, students work with the person who has signed up for that appointment time.

In the illustration shown, if the teacher said, "Go to your four o'clock appointment," the student would work with Ryan.

Figure 2.2   Appointments

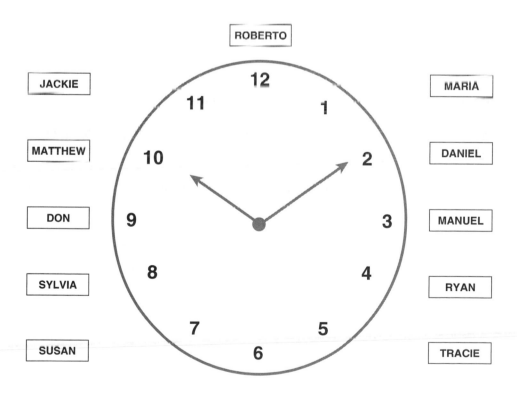

Line Up

A quick and easy way to put students into temporary groups is called Line Up. This method is limited only by our imagination in ways to ask students to line up. Some examples to get you started include the following:

Line up by

- The beginning letter of your last name

- Your shoe size

- How you feel about something—such as a school rule or item in the newspaper

- How well you understand a concept

- Your birthday, beginning with January 1

- The number of people in your immediate family

- Answers to math problems, from lowest to highest

- Your favorite literature characters

- Your birth order—first child, middle child, only child, last child

- Where you were born, from farthest away to the closest

After students line up, place them in groups of three or four by having them count off or fold the line over so that students are facing each other, and place them in groups of two with the person they are facing. A variation is to ask students to form two circles facing each other, then ask the outside circle to move three people to the right and place students in groups with the person they are facing.

INTEGRATING TECHNOLOGY AS A TOOL FOR BUILDING COMMUNITY

If you are in a school that is technologically savvy, you are way ahead of the game in being able to get your students plugged in. Use programs such as Go to Meeting or Google My Space to set up groups in your classroom where the students can talk to each other anytime through their personal chat sites. Place students in groups of three or four for the semester to serve as small learning communities. Through technology, older students can talk to each other about the assignments, questions, and prompts from you or just keep each other informed about the classroom work. Remember, this is the way that our students conduct conversations on a daily basis—digital is their first language.

Plugging In is about creating an environment that is inviting, rigorous rather than frustrating, and that follows the way today's students learn. It is about understanding that the students that we are teaching today learn visually first. Their brains have been wired from birth in an environment that is high tech, highly visual, and constantly changing. They communicate daily with their peers through pods, webs, chat rooms, blogs, and other digital devices. Instead of trying to force them back into a paradigm that focuses on sitting, listening, and getting information from a single source, try using the tools most familiar to them. In a school in Tennessee, we began a very successful program through which students helped teachers add technology to their lessons. Most of us speak digital as a second language; our students are digital natives. Let them help you learn the language.

SUMMARY

Plugging In is about creating the kind of environment that raises the comfort level of students. It is about a classroom that accepts everyone and provides everything possible to make him or her successful. There are no negative surprises. Students know what they must do to be successful, and if they do these things—they are successful. It does not matter who their mother is or whether their siblings did well in school; it doesn't even matter what they did last year or last semester in your classroom. We know from research that the following factors are critical to student success:

1. *They need self-efficacy.* Self-efficacy is the belief that I can be successful because I have been successful in the past. It is far more powerful than self-esteem because it is built on fact. Self-esteem says, "I feel good about myself." Self-efficacy says, "I know I can do this math because I have been successful at math before." If you teach students from poverty, especially inner-city poverty, this is critical. McCune, Stephens, and Lowe (1999) say that students usually attribute their success or failure to one or more of the following: ability ("I'm just not smart"), effort (I tried really hard"), task difficulty ("That test was too hard"), or luck ("I guessed right"). Generational poverty tends to blame failure on bad luck or some cloud that seems to hover over the family. For these students it is important that they experience success, even incrementally, so that they can break this cycle of failure and the belief system that feeds it.

2. *They need a nonthreatening environment.* Don't mistake this for a watered down curriculum. Learners don't feel good about themselves or the learning if they feel that it has been diluted for them. This is about creating an environment that says, "This classroom is made up of a community of learners, including the teacher, and together we are going to tackle the learning." It means that it is OK to fail; just not

OK not to try. Digital learners learn through trial and error; give them that opportunity in the classroom.

3. *They need to believe that they have everything that they need to be successful.* This means that they know from the beginning what is required and expected. For older students, it can be in writing. It means that they are given adequate time and directions so that they can be successful. It means that the learning is about understanding rather than covering the material.

4. *They need to see the personal relevance in the learning*—what does this learning have to do with them personally?

These factors are not equally weighted. A student might say, "I don't know when I would ever use the principle of how to figure slope in my daily life, but I like the classroom and I have had success here before, so I will hang in there and give the teacher a chance to show me the relevance." An elementary student might think, "I don't like science, but I like my teacher and the learning is fun, so I will see what my teacher is going to show me in science."

Using Figure 2.3, rate your comfort in using Plugging In for your classroom.

Figure 2.3   Rating Your Confidence Level for Plugging In

Rate your confidence in strategies to help your students plug into the learning	Yes	No
1. I make sure that my students feel welcome and confident in my classroom.		
2. I make sure that all of my students call each other by name.		
3. I provide opportunities for my students to interact with one another.		
4. I provide opportunities for all of my students to be successful.		
5. I provide enough information and practice time so that my students can be successful.		
6. I always tell my students up front what they must do to be successful.		
7. I use feedback often in my classroom.		
8. I help my students to see the personal relevance to the learning.		

WHAT DOES THE RESEARCH SAY?

Marzano (1998) wrote about the meta-analysis studies conducted at the Mid-continent Research Educational Laboratories. These studies showed that strategies used in the classroom to enhance the self-system of the brain had an overall effect size of .74, which translates to 27 percentile points.

For example, when teachers provided guided, focused, and accurate feedback to students about accomplishing tasks, the effect size was .74 (27 percentile points). When students worked in cooperative groups, as opposed to having to compete with others or to work alone, the effect size was .78 (28 percentile points). When teachers reinforced self-efficacy in students, the effect size was .80 (29 percentile points).

3

Powering Up

As a teacher, you cannot give meaning to another; the learner's brain must construct the meaning.

—Eric Jensen (1997, p. 32)

Most of us were trained to teach to the cognitive system of the brain; not much was said about teaching to the self-system or the metacognitive system. This fact contributes greatly to the lack of interest or motivation in many classrooms today.

All learning begins, not in the cognitive system, but in the self-system. It happens with or without our input. And it is more likely that our students will be motivated to learn and to complete tasks when we are directly involved in the learning process from the beginning. Marzano (2001) says, "Once the self-system has determined what will be attended to, the functioning of all other elements of thought (i.e., the metacognitive system, the cognitive system, and the knowledge domains) are, to a certain extent, dedicated or determined."

Let's look at a typical classroom as students come in for the class. As the room fills, some students are sitting quietly thinking, some are looking out the window or reading, some are talking boisterously, and some are visiting with friends in the classroom. They bring with them the problems from the hallway and their homes and with their class work. Some may be sleepy, some angry, some sad, and some just plain "bummed out" mentally. Their thoughts are on anything but the work ahead. And we are supposed to stand before them and lead them into the lesson for the day!

Figure 3.1   Strategic Learning Model: Powering Up

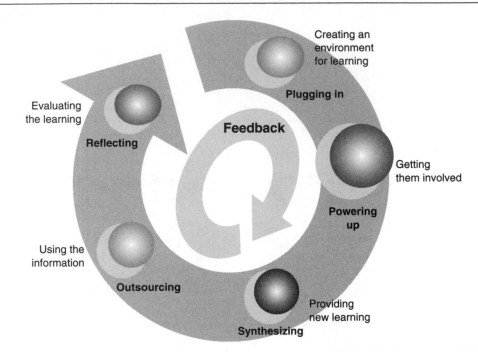

BEGINNING WITH THE SELF-SYSTEM OF THE BRAIN

The self-system is a prime determiner in the motivation that is brought to a new task. It is not a specific place in the brain but is made up of a system of interrelated "attitudes, beliefs, and emotions." It is the interaction of these attitudes, beliefs and emotions that determines both motivation and attention. Specifically, the self-system determines whether an individual will engage in or disengage in a given task; it also determines how much energy the individual will bring to the task (Marzano, 2001, p. 50). This means that to be motivated, a set of beliefs must be in place. As a teacher, I need to establish the importance of the learning and make a connection between what my students already know and the new knowledge. In Chapter 2 we discussed four important factors that assist the brain in making the decision to pay attention. To recap from the point of view of the learner, they are

1. The belief that I can be successful because I have been successful in the past

2. A positive feeling about the learning, the classroom, the teacher and peers; emotion is thought to be the strongest force in the brain. Negative emotion can literally shut down thought processes while positive emotions can help shape our motivation to learn. Don't believe me? Next time you lose your car keys, see if you can do higher-level math in your emotional state. The emotional response that a student brings to a new task will help shape the degree of motivation associated with that task. This is just one of the reasons that it is important to have a positive learning environment prior to teaching the lesson. A positive learning environment includes both the physical and

emotional structures in place. A warm and caring teacher who has no consistency or planning will have difficulty in terms of student progress.

3. The tools to be successful, which include something in writing telling me what is expected, appropriate instruction, enough time to practice, and the opportunity to ask questions

4. The belief that the learning is important, that it is worth my time and effort

MIND JOGS

As a teacher, what can you do at the beginning of a lesson to provide nourishment to your students' self-systems? One of the activities that I often use in my classrooms—even with my college students—is a tool called Mind Jogs.

Mind jogs are activities that emphasize higher-level thinking and creativity. Class begins the moment students walk into the classroom; it doesn't matter if the bell has rung. They begin with a mind jog activity. It might be on the overhead, on PowerPoint on the computer, handed to them as they enter the room, or assigned in the previous class. Mind jogs are always high level, interesting, and meaningful. Two examples are

- Mission Possible
- Where Are You?

Mission Possible

Three of our top agents are suspects in a scam to sell arms to Third World countries. Two of the agents have been trained to always lie when questioned, whereas the third always tells the truth.

- Agent 1 says he did not sell arms to Third World countries.

- Agent 2 says he is the one who sold the arms to Third World countries.

- Agent 3 says that Agent 2 did not sell arms to Third World countries.

Your mission, should you decide to take it (and I know you will), is to find which of the three agents sold the arms. Be able to prove your answer.

Answer: Agent 1 sold them. Because Agent 2 and Agent 3 contradict each other, one of them must be telling the truth. Because either Agent 1 or Agent 2 is the only truth teller, Agent 1 must be a liar. Therefore, Agent 1 is the seller.

I like this activity because it is a good introduction to problem solving and to solving for an unknown.

Where Are You?

Directions: From the clues given, can you guess, "Where are you?"

- Sitting Bull is buried in this state. Where are you?

- Jefferson is 60 feet tall. Name the state and the place.

- Teachers: Produce pictures of recognizable geographical places, such as Mount Rushmore, for students to determine the name of the monument and the location.

BUILDING CONNECTIONS

Another key part of Powering Up is to tap into students' prior knowledge and to build a bridge between what students already know and the new information.

Thanks to brain research and the use of MRI, we now know that the brain is a seeker of connections. When new information is given to us without any connection in the brain, there is chaos until a connection is made. Sometimes this is referred to as a *schema* or framework for the brain. We often make false assumptions about what students already know.

Ask yourself, "What do students already know?" What existing frameworks do they already have?" As the student, if I do not understand that the underlying principle behind algebra is solving for an unknown, I will experience confusion as the teacher moves through the lesson using symbols such as x and y. A lesson in immigration will have more meaning to me if I think about why people leave their homeland and often risk their lives to come to a place where they may not know anyone. As the teacher introducing such a lesson, ask your students, "What would have to happen in your life to cause you to go to another country to live?"

With young children for a lesson on the explorers, you might ask, "Have you ever gone on a trip to a place you had never visited before? What did you expect to find? Were you surprised by what you saw or heard? Did you get tired before you got there?"

Students are not simply passive receivers waiting to be supplied with the correct information; they come to tasks with their own knowledge and expectations. Distortions in recall often occur when new information doesn't fit in an existing schema. We forget or distort aspects that are incompatible with our schemas. Ask, "What misconceptions do my students have?"

The best gift that a teacher can give to those students who traditionally have not done well in school is a hook or framework for the new information so that confusion is eliminated in the brain.

Techniques for tapping into prior learning and for providing a framework for new learning include the following:

- KNLH (Know, Need to Know, Learned, How Did You Learn It?)
- Group Memory
- Using a Matrix 1: Helping Students Think Out of the Box
- Making Predictions
- Before and After

KNLH (Know, Need to Know, Learned, How Did You Learn It?)

Before the lesson, the teacher uses direct questioning to determine what students know about the content from prior instruction and personal experience. The teacher may guide the students to categorize the information they have generated. For example, for a lesson on immigration, a teacher might ask students what would cause them to leave this country and go live in a country where they knew no one. Next, the teacher might ask students to think of their answers in categories such as the following:

- What would have to happen in this country on the religious front?
- Economically?
- Medically?
- Socially?
- Politically?

This is an opportunity to correct misconceptions students may have about the information to be studied. This technique may also be used to build interest in the topic. Putting the information in the same categories that will be used throughout the unit of study helps students to create a pattern for better understanding.

Next, direct the students to think about what they *need to know*. Ask them to come up with questions they have about what they are about to study. Teachers may want to take the lists from each group and combine them into a class list. The list should be displayed so that the class can refer to it throughout the lesson.

After the lesson, the students evaluate what they have *learned* and *how* they learned it. This is also an opportunity for the teacher to evaluate whether the lesson has answered student questions and misconceptions. It is important for students to think about how they learned the information as it can serve as a guide to them as they become more independent learners, relying less on the teacher as their source of information. See Table 3.1 for a sample chart layout for this activity.

Table 3.1   KWHL (Know, Need to Know, Learned, How Did You Learn It?)

Know	Want to Know	Learned	How Did You Learn It?

Group Memory

For this activity, students are placed into groups of three. The teacher assigns the topic and gives students the following six-step directions:

1. Write everything you know about the topic.

2. Discuss what you have written with your group.

3. List individual questions that you have about the subject.

4. Share the information with the group. You may write down anything you hear.

5. Compile group questions. Share with the class. A class list should be posted on chart paper or on the board.

6. After the lesson, check questions that were posted earlier.

Suggestions for Use

- Prior to studying a historical event, such as the Boston Tea Party

- Prior to a unit in science, such as heredity

- Prior to a lesson in math, such as on quadrilaterals

- Prior to a lesson in literature, such as on *Hiroshima*, by John Hersey (1985), ask, "What do you know about the atomic bomb used in World War II?"

Reasons for Using

- Helps to clarify what students know

- Gives the teacher an opportunity to correct false information

- Enhances collaborative skills

- Ties the learning to prior knowledge and to prior questions

Using a Matrix 1: Helping Students Think Out of the Box

This activity is an extension of brainstorming and helps students to think "out of the box." The teacher announces the topic, and students are asked to brainstorm within their groups. Next, students are asked to put their answers into categories.

Suggestions for Use

This technique can be used in any phase of a lesson. In the personal connection phase, it is used to help students identify with the new knowledge they are about to receive. For example, before a study on hunger, ask students to brainstorm reasons they believe hunger is a problem in the United States. Next, ask them to plot the information on a matrix in categories such as political reasons, social reasons, economic reasons, and so forth.

Because students often brainstorm ideas that are similar, they can be asked to combine their answers into categories. The teacher should provide the categories until students are very adept at this skill; then, they may form their own categories.

Reasons for Using

- Helps students see information from various points of view
- Enhances the learning for visual learners
- Develops higher-level thinking skills
- Teaches analysis

Table 3.2   Sample Matrix 1

	Political	Economic	Social
Urban areas			
Suburban areas			
Intercity			
Rural areas			

Making Predictions

Comprehension is affected by anticipation. Teachers can do a great deal to set the stage for expecting and predicting meaning. A three-step process for group prediction activities follows:

1. In their study groups, the students read aloud the title of the lesson and several paragraphs about it.

2. The teacher identifies a place in the reading or lesson for predictions.

3. Students work in partners to predict what will happen next.

Suggestions for Use

Groups make written predications about the lesson based on questions given by the teacher. For example, for the short story *After Twenty Years*, by O. Henry, the teacher might read the opening paragraphs and ask the class to discuss with a partner what kinds of questions they might ask of each other if they met again after 20 years.

In science class, students might read the background information on a new unit and make predictions about the experiments they will perform. In math class, students make predictions about how to solve the problems studied.

Reasons for Using

- To arouse curiosity and to make the learning more meaningful

- To heighten awareness of the process

Before and After

The Before and After exercise is another version of Making Predictions. In this exercise, students must follow up their predictions to determine if their prior knowledge was correct. See Table 3.3 for an example.

Table 3.3   Before and After

Directions: Before reading, place a check in the True box in the before-reading column if you believe the statement is true; place a check in the False box if you believe the statement is false. After you have finished the unit, check to see if your answers were correct.

	Before Reading			After Reading	
	True	False	Statement	True	False
1.			World War II began with the invasion of Poland.		
2.			The Axis Powers were Germany, Italy, and France.		
3.			The Soviet Union signed a treaty with Hitler but entered the war on the side of the Allies.		
4.			The United States entered the war at its beginning.		
5.			The defeated countries were given less punitive punishment at the end of World War II than at the end of World War I.		

Answers: 1, 3, and 5 are true; 2 and 4 are false.

SUMMARY

Powering Up is the point in the lesson when we pull students into the learning by tapping into what they already know and by creating a hook to the new learning. About 98% of all new learning comes to us through the senses—all of the senses. Use all of the senses to gain access to your students' brains. Stand at the doorway of your classroom. What does your room look like? What is there that will help your visual students to learn and understand? Visual learners need to see the learning for it to make sense; just hearing is not enough. If you teach math, do you have visual representatives of the learning? What does your room smell like? Remember from Chapter 2 that how we feel about the place where we are learning is important. If you are studying France, just bringing in some of the smells of France, such as croissants or lavender, will help your students to remember the learning. Why? The brain likes context, and it will attach the memory to the smell or context of the learning. What does your room sound like? Who is doing all of the talking? Do you use sound for teaching? My brother is a scientist today, and he tells me that everything he ever needed to know in life, he learned in second grade. His teacher was wonderful. He said that if they were studying Italy, their room was Italy: It smelled like Italy, it sounded like Italy, and it looked like Italy. His first love and appreciation for opera came from this classroom. His love of science came from this classroom because students were allowed to explore and find answers for themselves.

Who wouldn't want their child to be in a classroom like this? What do you have in your classroom for students to touch? Or what do you do to encourage your students to explore, to move and to have an opportunity to do more than sit passively? Power Up is about powering up the excitement of learning.

Using Table 3.4, rate how comfortable you are with powering up your classroom.

Table 3.4   Rating Your Confidence Level for Powering Up

Rate your confidence in strategies to help your students get involved in the learning	Yes	No
1. I have activities for my students during that time before the bell rings to begin the lessons.		
2. I have structures already in place for students to work together in teams, in pairs or in threes.		
3. I have given my students clear instructions on the expectations for the learning.		
4. I make sure that my students have everything that they need to be successful.		
5. I understand and utilize the self system of the brain.		
6. I use graphs and models to help my students tap into the learning.		
7. I use feedback often in my classroom.		
8. I help my students to see the personal relevance to the learning.		

WHAT DOES THE RESEARCH SAY?

The meta-analysis studies conducted by McREL (Marzano, 1998) show the following:
When the goal of the learning is to help students to understand their own self-attributes and those of their peers, the important strategies that have the highest effect on this phase of the learning appear to be the following:

1. Providing opportunities for students to verbalize their thinking concerning their belief systems about themselves and others; the effect size for the studies was 1.38 or 41 percentile points.

2. Helping students to understand the connections between beliefs and behaviors

3. Leading students to understand how to change behaviors

When students were led to understand the connection between their beliefs and their behavior and then helped to change behaviors, the effect size was .89 (31 percentile points).

4

Synthesizing

I am a part of all that I have known

—Tennyson

Once the climate has been established in the classroom and structures are in place for collaboration, the teacher is ready to help students move into the cognitive areas of the learning. Cognitive information is usually thought of as either declarative (information, facts, rules, and heuristics) or procedural (processes using the information from the declarative). Students, even young children, should be told what the purpose of the lesson is and what they will be doing. Older students should be given the information in writing, either by putting it up somewhere in the classroom or by providing that information to each student individually in print or online. Why is this so important?

THE METACOGNITIVE SYSTEM

The metacognitive system of the brain is that system that causes us to make a plan for carrying out our learning. Anytime we are given a task, this system comes into play as we determine how we will tackle the work. As anyone knows who has ever attempted to put toys together on Christmas Eve, plans do not always work out as we thought. It is the metacognitive system that determines whether we will monitor and adjust at those times or throw up our hands and give up. In fact, the decision to readjust and try another way is one of the attributes that we equate with smart and successful people. They don't give up.

Children who have been raised in an environment of poverty often acquiesce at the first sign of a problem. We want to model for our students how to plan for

Figure 4.1   Strategic Learning Model: Synthesizing

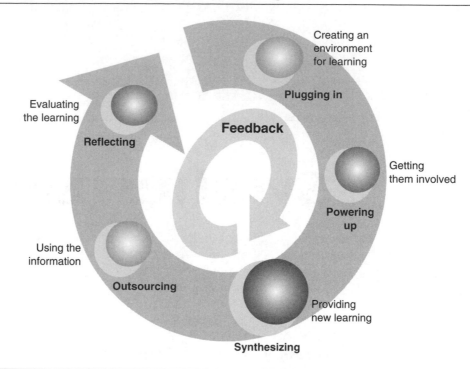

declarative information (facts) and for procedural learning (processes). We want to show them how to use positive self-talk by showing them what we do when we can't get the answer to the problem or can't pronounce the vocabulary word.

Ask students to write or discuss their own goals for the learning. The KNLH tool that you used in the previous chapter is one example of a way to get students thinking about what they want to learn. Using learning logs is another effective way to do this.

BUILDING DECLARATIVE KNOWLEDGE

Synthesizing includes all of the strategies that are used to help students acquire declarative information. Whether the classroom is housed in an elementary school or a secondary school, synthesizing emphasizes a curriculum of substance in which

- Students are required to do serious work.
- Instructional strategies that engage students and make them part of the learning process are the rule, not the exception.
- There is a climate supportive of teaching and learning.
- Technology is a part of the teaching and learning and goes far beyond drill and practice or the use of PowerPoint.
- Learning is based on brain research.
- Multiple resources are used.
- Lecture is limited to the age of the learner (e.g., 5 minutes for 5-year-olds).
- Collaboration is encouraged and the classroom is a community of learners together.

What are the implications for the traditional lecture approach to teaching? If we, as teachers, learned our subject best when we began teaching it, what is the implication for allowing students to work together to teach each other, to share information, and to practice the learning?

What is the implication of memorizing facts for a test and then forgetting them afterward, as opposed to making the learning meaningful so that students will not forget? Techniques that encourage synthesizing include the following:

1. Bookends

2. Think, Pair, Share

3. Pairs to Squares

4. Expert Groups

5. Numbered Heads Together

6. Scavenger Hunt

7. Six Thinking Hats

Bookends

Bookends is a technique from cooperative learning that is a good beginning for those teachers who are reluctant to give up lectures. It incorporates short lecture segments with frequent breaks for students to assimilate the information.

The directions are these six steps:

1. Students focus on the teacher.

2. The teacher gives information to the class for 15 minutes or less.

3. The students discuss the information in pairs.

4. The teacher gives the students additional information for 15 minutes or less.

5. The students discuss the new information.

6. The teacher assigns a task for the class.

Suggestions for Use

- Any time new information is being introduced
- To help break down complex information

Reasons for Using

- To help students assimilate new information
- To teach students to teach information to each other so that the information is internalized

Think, Pair, Share

This is another cooperative learning technique that helps students give meaning to the information they receive.

Directions:

- Students listen while the teacher poses a question.
- Students are given time to think of a response. (Variation: Students write a response.)
- Students turn to a partner and discuss their responses.
- Groups share their responses with the class.

How and When to Use

- For those times when you want to give a great deal of information to the class but you want to do it with a minimum of lecture
- During class discussion so that all students have an opportunity to participate
- After a new concept has been introduced, to provide opportunities for clarification

Example: For a unit on hunger, the teacher might say, "In this country, we produce enough food for every man, woman, and child in the world to have 2,100 calories a day. Why, then, are people hungry?"

1. Students are given time to think of a response.

2. Students would share their ideas with their partners or their study group.

3. Groups would share their ideas with the class.

Pairs to Squares

Pairs to Squares is a variation of Think, Pair, Share. The two steps are these:

1. Students discuss problems, write answers to questions, and work on problems in pairs.

2. Each pair turns to another pair (to make a square) to check their answers. If the two sets of answers are not the same, the square must discuss until one answer is agreed on.

How and When to Use

- In any subject where there are many steps involved in the solution

- For creative problem solving

- For making predictions; a consensus would not be necessary here as long as the students could give reasons for their predictions. The purpose would be to foster thinking and reasoning abilities.

- To edit and elaborate writing: Each pair writes and the square edits or elaborates or both.

- To check homework

Expert Groups

Expert Groups is a variation of the cooperative learning technique called Jigsaw. The four steps are as follows:

1. Groups divide the work or information into smaller chunks according to the number in the group.

2. Each member is assigned one part of the material.

3. Members join members from other groups who have the same assignment and agree on what is important and how to teach the material to their respective learning groups.

4. Experts return to their learning groups to take turns teaching each other their parts of the assignment.

How and When to Use

- When students have a large amount of material to cover
- When the depth of learning is important
- To break down complicated information into chunks for understanding

Example: After reading the first half of Golding and Epstein's (1959) novel *Lord of the Flies,* students are placed in groups of five. Each person in the group is assigned a different character from the book and is given a list of questions about that character. Questions can include the following:

- What does your character look like?
- How does he feel about the other boys in the group?
- How do they feel about him?
- So far, what is his purpose in the story?

After the students have been given about 20 minutes to look up their answers, they move to the expert groups made up of other students in the class who have the same character. The expert groups compare notes and compile the best answers to the questions. The experts return to their original study groups to teach the information to the group. The teacher calls on students to speak to the class about their characters. Because the teacher calls on students randomly, all students must be prepared to be the spokesperson for their expert group. When called on, the spokesperson takes on the role of the assigned character. For example, the spokesperson for the character of Piggy would say, "My name is Piggy and this is what I think of the other boys with me: . . ."

This is a far better way to help students understand the characters than simply reading the novel and answering questions from a ditto. Remember that the objective is to put the information into long-term memory.

Numbered Heads Together

This is a great cooperative learning technique because it requires that everyone actively participate. The four steps are these:

1. In their regular study groups, students number off, 1 through 4.

2. Teacher announces a question and a time limit.

3. Students put their heads together and discuss answers to the question.

4. Teacher calls a number, and students with that number answer for their groups.

How and When to Use

- To master basic facts and as a test review

- At the knowledge and comprehension level of Bloom's Taxonomy

- As a group competition

- For assessment: Allow groups to make up their own review questions to be used by the teacher. Give bonus points for well-written questions that stump other groups.

Example: In the book *Math Curse,* by Jon Scieszka and Lane Smith (1995), Mrs. Fibonacci counts like this: 1, 1, 2, 3, 5, 8, 13. . . .

What are the next five numbers in Mrs. Fibonacci's counting system?

1. Students discuss the answer in their groups.

2. The students count off from 1 to 4. The teacher checks to see that all groups have done this.

3. The teacher randomly calls a number, such as "3." All of the students who have the designated number stand up. The teacher calls on one of them for the answer.

4. If the answer is correct, the students sit down, and the teacher asks another question. If the answer is incorrect, another student is asked to give the answer.

One of the advantages of this technique is that everyone must be alert at all times because no one knows who will be accountable for the answer. Another advantage is that when a student answers, the answer is not an individual one but the answer of the group, and there is less stigma about getting the answer wrong.

Are You Hungry? A Scavenger Hunt About Hunger in the United States

Rules for the hunt:

1. You must work in groups of four, with each member contributing equally to the whole group effort.

2. You can go anywhere that is appropriate to obtain your data. Cameras and tape recorders may be used to record information. Written summaries of television shows, hand-drawn maps and diagrams are acceptable.

3. Use primary sources when possible.

4. The sources of all data must be recorded.

Items to collect and create:

- Collect three to five articles about poverty in the United States. Be sure that they cover more than one category (homelessness, unemployment, overpopulation, etc.).

- Chart how the United States spends money to help the poor in our country.

- Collect at least five songs that have the theme of poverty. Share the lyrics in some unique way with the class.

- On a map of the United States, locate the five areas that contain the largest number of people in poverty. Research the reasons why.

- Chart a matrix on how overpopulation, hunger, and poverty can affect the environment.

- Find out the number of homeless and unemployed in your community. Chart or graph your findings.

- Mind map the causes of poverty. (A mind map is a graph that helps the brain make visual connections between thoughts, ideas, words, or pictures.)

- Create a list of things that individuals can do to help alleviate poverty in their community or their country.

Six Thinking Hats

Edward DeBono (1985) wrote a wonderful book titled *Six Thinking Hats*. The book was written to help people in business and industry break out of their traditional thinking so that problems and innovations could be approached from a fresh direction. The ideas work well in the classroom, where we so often get cookie-cutter-type ideas from students. Another advantage to using this technique in the classroom is that it is a nonthreatening way to get usually negatively thinking students to think in another direction. Because they are playing a role in the activity, the technique is not threatening.

How to Use in the Classroom

Assign each group in the classroom a different hat. Based on the definition of the hat, the group approaches the assignment only from the viewpoint of the hat they have been given. For our lesson on hunger, the assignments might be thus:

1. *Group 1: White Hat Thinking.* This group looks only at the facts about hunger in the United States. They are not concerned with "I think" or "I feel" perspectives, only with data.

2. *Group 2: Red Hat Thinking.* This group is concerned with hunches and feelings about the problem of hunger in the United States. These hunches do not have to be backed by hard data. The members will report their opinions about the problem.

3. *Group 3: Black Hat Thinking.* This group will report all of the reasons why efforts to end hunger in the United States will not work. Their answers will be based on logic from a negative viewpoint.

4. *Group 4: Yellow Hat Thinking.* This group will report all the reasons that efforts to feed the poor will work. They will focus on the benefits of the efforts to end hunger and the constructive thinking that can make it happen.

5. *Group 5: Green Hat Thinking.* This group will focus on the innovative ideas that are being considered to end hunger. Their emphasis will be creative, new, and innovative approaches.

6. *Group 6: Blue Hat Thinking.* This group will be responsible for the organization of the project. They will manage the other groups to see that they are on target and that they have the tools they need to complete their tasks. This group will also be responsible for the evaluation of the project and for tying all of the thinking together.

7. In the first few projects that I do with this model, as the teacher, I am the blue hat thinker. The maturity and expertise of your class will determine at what point students are ready to take on this role.

Variation

Frames of Reference. Groups are handed picture frames with specific words or ideas written on them, and the groups look at the information to be studied from those viewpoints. For example, the frames might be identified by Who, What, Where, How, and When. In the events leading up to World War II, *Who* were the key players, *What* events were significant, *Where* were the events taking place and what was the significance of the location, *How* were people reacting to the events, and *When* were the critical events taking place?

SUMMARY

Synthesizing is about learning declarative information from multiple sources and integrating it so that it is meaningful and useful to the student. Teachers who are good at helping students synthesize use a variety of teaching strategies, and they incorporate all of the learning modalities that we discussed in the previous chapter—seeing, hearing, smelling, touching, and tasting. This is differentiation in practice. These teachers use context, story telling, visual representations, and collaboration to reach all students. Using Table 4.1, check your comfort level in using synthesizing in your classroom.

Table 4.1   Rating Your Confidence Level for Synthesizing

Rate your confidence in strategies to help your students learn in a variety of contexts	Yes	No
1. I use visual models in my classroom.		
2. I limit lecture to the age of my students: 10 minutes for 10-year-olds, etc.		
3. I teach information in context.		
4. I am a part of the learning community of my classroom.		
5. I provide enough information and practice time so that my students can be successful.		
6. I always tell my students up front what they must do to be successful.		
7. I often use feedback in my classroom.		
8. I use movement in my classroom.		

WHAT DOES THE RESEARCH SAY?

The research from McREL (Marzano, 1998) on 135 studies shows the following:

Using cues (brief previews of the information or skills that are to be addressed in the lesson) has an effect size of 1.13, which raises achievement by 37 percentile points.

Using questions prior to a lesson to determine the learning level of students and then throughout the lesson raises the learning level by .93 or 32 percentile points.

Using direct schema by asking students what they know about a topic prior to studying that topic has an effect size of .75 or 27 percentile points.

5

Outsourcing

Learning is an active process in which meaning is developed on the basis of experience.

—Duffey and Jonassen (1992)

At this point in the lesson, students are given the opportunity to demonstrate understanding by using the information they have learned in some way. Students who learn best by tactile or visual means need the opportunity to use graphic or concrete models to help solidify the information. Concrete models are some of the best gifts that we can give to the learners at this point, particularly the visual learners. The word *concrete* is not used by accident—concrete models help to put ideas in concrete for the student.

A variety of concrete models will be demonstrated in this section. They include the following:

1. Collaborative Retelling
2. Alike and Different
3. Fat and Skinny Questions
4. Attribute Webs
5. Mindmaps
6. Thinking at Right Angles
7. Using a Matrix 2
8. Fishbone
9. Venn Diagrams

Figure 5.1   Strategic Learning Model: Outsourcing

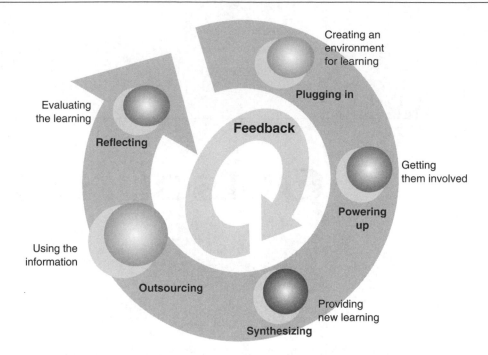

CONCRETE MODELS

What Are Concrete Models?

Concrete models are visual representatives of the learning. They are mental maps to help students understand and remember difficult concepts, such as sequencing, comparing and contrasting, and classifying. Some writers, such as Marzano (2001), divide concrete models into three types:

1. Advance Organizers: Models used to help students organize information and to introduce new learning in advance of the new learning—hence the name "advance organizers."

2. Linguistic Organizers: Models that rely on words more than form to convey their messages; a learning log would be an example of a linguistic organizer. In a learning log, the teacher gives a prompt to the students for writing in their logs. Prior to a lesson on the weather, a teacher might ask students to write about their favorite kinds of weather or their experience with storms. The teacher is using the tool to tap into the students' prior learning and to hook them into the learning. During a lesson, the teacher might ask the students to write in their logs about information that they have learned. The teacher might ask, "In our lesson today, we have been talking about what causes storms. If you were explaining storms to someone not in this class, what would you say? Write this in your learning log." At the end of the lesson, the teacher might say, "Now that you know more about storms and what

causes them, will this change the way that you feel about them? Write your thinking in your learning log."

3. Nonlinguistic Organizers: Models that rely on their visual representation as much as or more than words to convey meaning; a mindmap is considered to be a nonlinguistic organizer.

Why Use Concrete Models?

Concrete models help students connect or relate new information to prior knowledge. Because they make abstract ideas more visible, they help students understand and remember concepts that are difficult to visualize otherwise. Students who are visual learners need concrete models to help them organize and process information.

When Do We Use Concrete Models?

Concrete models can be used at any time during the learning process but are critical in the phase of the lesson in which the teacher wants the students to use the new information in some way. This is a time for clarifying ideas, for both the student and the teacher, prior to assessment. Other times in which concrete models might be used include the following:

- When introducing a difficult or abstract concept: If I want students to understand how to effectively compare and contrast two things, I might use a graphic model, such as the one shown in Figure 5.2. In this model, students list on the top lines how the two things are alike. Then on the bottom half of the model, students tell how they are different according to the attributes that are important. For example, if I were comparing Lincoln and Douglass, an attribute that would be important to use for contrasting would be their styles of debate. Their economic backgrounds would not be an important attribute because they were both from poor families.
- When assessing the learning: A friend of mine helps prepare students for the Scholastic Aptitude Test for college entrance. She tells me that she often tests her students' understanding by having them mindmap information. She says it is a great way to quickly find out their thinking. They either know the information or they do not; they cannot bluff their way through with words. Try using concrete models as part of your daily formative assessments. If you teach young elementary students, you can do mindmaps by having students glue pictures to the mindmaps.
- As part of an individual or group project: Building in concrete models as a part of the assignment is a good way to get students using the maps. There are several software packages that help students to create concrete models.
- To demonstrate understanding of a concept: In order to use concrete models appropriately, I have to understand the concept that I am demonstrating. Asking students to show you their learning in a concrete model is a way to see quickly if they understand and is a lead-in to constructive feedback.
- To demonstrate creativity: Provide general directions to your students for doing concrete models, but allow them to add their own creativity to the process or to come up with their own models.

Figure 5.2   A Graphic Model to Compare and Contrast

	Lincoln	*Douglass*
How Alike?		
How Different With Regard to		
First characteristic		
Second characteristic		
Third characteristic		
Fourth characteristic		

Collaborative Retelling

Collaborative Retelling reinforces the learning by giving students opportunities to repeat the information learned. This is also a technique that encourages elaboration because students are prompted to remember details.

Students are placed into groups of two. The five steps are as follows:

1. The teacher hands out the Collaborative Retelling sheet to each pair of students (see Table 5.1 for an example).

2. Students number off so that there is a Student 1 and a Student 2.

3. Student 1 asks Student 2 to tell everything he or she remembers about the lesson. As ideas are mentioned, Student 1 puts a check mark in the "First Retelling" column.

4. When Student 2 is finished, Student 1 uses clues to help Student 2 remember details not mentioned. Student 1 checks off items Student 2 is able to elaborate on.

Table 5.1   Collaborative Retelling for *After Twenty Years* by O'Henry

First Retelling	Clued Retelling	Ideas
		The promise
		The setting
		The lamppost
		The policeman
		The cigarette
		The betrayal

Alike and Different

This model can be used for any subject for which students need to make comparisons. Before students can compare, they must understand attributes. This is a beginning step for more difficult comparing and contrasting activities.

At the beginning level, teachers give the categories. As students learn to think in flexible terms, they can add their own categories. See Table 5.2 for an example.

Table 5.2   "Alike and Different" Example

	Clinton	*Dole*
How Alike?		
How Different With Regard to		
Education policy		
Foreign policy		
Tax cuts		
Medicare		

Fat and Skinny Questions

Fat questions require lots of discussion and explanation with interesting examples. Fat questions take time to think through and answer in depth.

Skinny questions require simple "yes," "no," or "maybe" answers.

Ways to Use

Ask students to make up five fat questions and five skinny questions about a lesson.

Reasons for Using

- Teaches collaborative skills
- Increases awareness of in-depth questioning

For examples, see Table 5.3.

Table 5.3   Fat and Skinny Questions

Directions: In the column for Fat questions, list questions that cannot be answered by "yes" or "no" or with one-word answers. Under the column for Skinny questions, list questions that can be answered with one-word answers.

	Fat?	Skinny?
1.	What were the events that led to World War II?	When did World War II begin?
2.	How was Hitler able to rise to power in Germany?	When did the United States enter the war?
3.	Why didn't the United States enter the war before Pearl Harbor?	Who was President of the United States during the war?
4.	Compare and contrast Winston Churchill and Franklin D. Roosevelt.	Who were the Allies?
5.	What were the agreements reached at Yalta?	Who attacked the United States at Pearl Harbor?

BRAINSTORMING MODELS

Brainstorming is a way to get many ideas before the class. The emphasis is on quantity. As the teacher, you will want to encourage all students to participate and share their ideas on the subject. To encourage this free flow of ideas, basic rules must be established before the brainstorming session. The following is a suggested set:

Rules for Brainstorming

- Accept all ideas without judgment—one person's ideas may lead to other ideas.
- Look for as many ideas as you can—the emphasis is on quantity at this point.
- Make yourself stretch for new ideas—common ideas are usually offered first. Wait for a pause in the flow of ideas because the most creative ideas usually come after it.
- Seek combinations of ideas and use the ideas of others to expand to new ones—this is one of those times when using others' ideas is encouraged.

Mindmaps and Attribute Webs, whose descriptions follow, are brainstorming models.

Mindmaps

Mindmaps are visual pictures of the learning. They provide a way to show a great deal of information in a small space. The main idea is written in the center box, with subordinating ideas in the surrounding circles. Additional ideas about the subordinating ideas are written in boxes that extend from the circles.

Variation

Ask students to prove their information with page numbers from the text or other sources in the subordinating ideas circles (see Figure 5.3.)

Figure 5.3   A Sample Mindmap

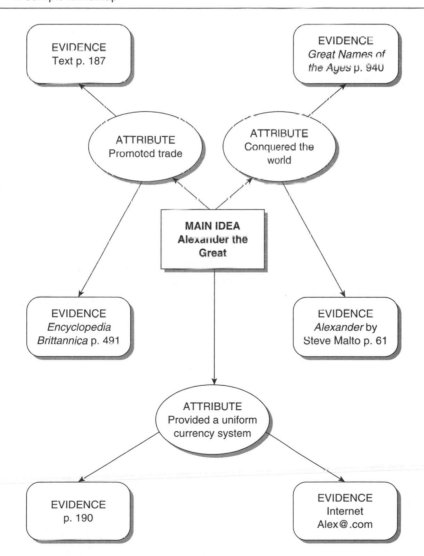

Attribute Webs

An attribute web is a variation of the mindmap. It is a way to show attributes in a concrete form. A web begins with a main idea, and attributes of that idea are placed on the spokes coming from the main idea.

For example, ask students to analyze the attributes of their study of Alexander the Great. The name *Alexander the Great* is placed in the center of the web, and attributes of Alexander the Great are written on the lines extending from the center of the web. This is a good beginning activity for higher-level thinking models, such as comparing and contrasting or for making Venn diagrams.

This is also a good beginning activity for writing reports or for research projects because it requires students to break down a complex topic into smaller parts. See Figure 5.4 for an example.

Figure 5.4   A Sample Attribute Web

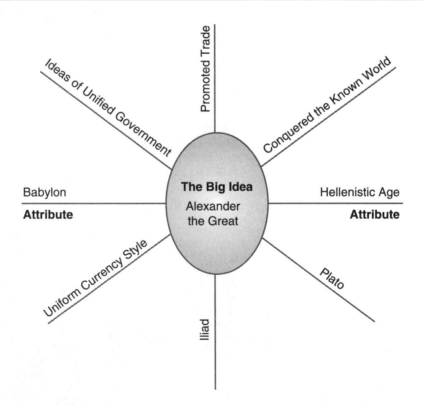

THINKING IN CATEGORIES

This section explores ways to help students (a) expand their thinking by looking at information in various ways, (b) approach problems from different directions, and (c) look at information from many points of view. Included in this section are the following activities:

- Thinking at Right Angles
- Using a Matrix 2
- Fishbone
- Venn Diagrams

Thinking at Right Angles

This activity helps students to associate ideas and to expand ideas into new categories.

For example, ask students to list, on the right side of the angle, characteristics of a character they have been studying. On the left arrow, write ideas that come to you as you list characteristics. This might include personal experiences, other people with this characteristic, and so forth.

In Table 5.4, information about the people killed in the Holocaust was given on the horizontal side of the angle. The student wrote thoughts about the information on the vertical side of the angle.

Table 5.4   Thinking at Right Angles—Example: The Holocaust

Directions: Fill in the mindmap using concrete evidence from your text or other sources.

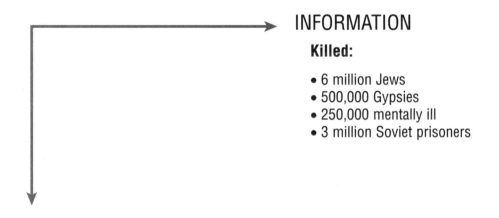

INFORMATION

Killed:

- 6 million Jews
- 500,000 Gypsies
- 250,000 mentally ill
- 3 million Soviet prisoners

MY THOUGHTS

- Why did it take so long for the United States to act?
- How was the Nazi regime able to carry out so many killings?

Using a Matrix 2

As mentioned in Chapter 4, using a matrix is a good way to get students to look at information from more than one point of view.

For example, you might give students a matrix with the names of countries studied going down the left column and categories such as population, currency, ethnicity, products, and greatest national problem written across the top cells. Students fill in the cells under the categories for each country.

This activity can be used at any point in the lesson cycle, including evaluation. See Table 5.5 for an example.

Table 5.5   Matrix 2

Country	Population	Currency	Products	Greatest Problem
Greece				
Italy				
France				
Spain				

Fishbone

A fishbone can be used when you want students to analyze information or as a first step in problem solving. The problem is written in the box, with each part of the fishbone representing a breakdown of the problem, such as who, what, when, where, how and why. Students analyze each of the subtopics to determine the cause of the problem. A fishbone is an analysis tool in which we know the end result and we want to know how we got to that result. It is a great beginning tool for teaching Systems Thinking.

Variation

Use as a visual representation of causes that led to an event. For example, place the words *World War II* in the box, and ask students to list causes in the bones of the fish (see Figure 5.5 for an example).

Figure 5.5   Fishbone Example

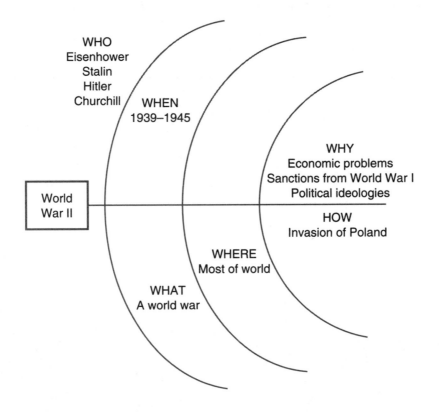

Venn Diagrams

Using Venn diagrams is an excellent way to help students see how things are alike and how they are different. A prerequisite to this kind of thinking is the ability to determine attributes.

For example, ask students to list attributes they have learned about World War I and World War II. Ask them to plot those ideas on a Venn diagram with the attributes that both share in the center and the individual attributes on the outer edges of the circles (see Figure 5.6 for an example).

Figure 5.6   Venn Diagram

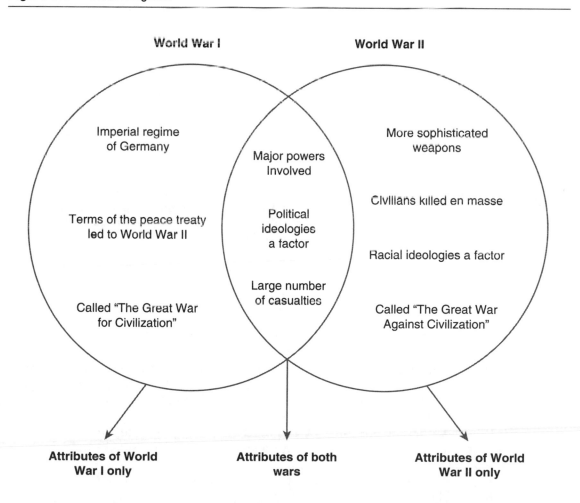

SUMMARY

Outsourcing is the place in the lesson where students use the information that they have learned in a meaningful way. Outsourcing might be done verbally, through visuals, or through movement or touch. In the ideal classroom, students are given choices for how they will demonstrate the learning. While that is not possible every day, it should be a part of the overall lesson scheme.

Using Table 5.6, rate your confidence in using Outsourcing in your classroom.

Table 5.6   Rating Your Confidence Level for Outsourcing

Rate your confidence in strategies to help your students use the new learning	*Yes*	*No*
1. I make sure that my students know how to use a variety of concrete models.		
2. I demonstrate for my students how to use concrete models.		
3. I provide many visuals in my classroom to help my students learn.		
4. I provide ample time for my students to practice the learning.		
5. I make sure that my students understand and can use the new learning before I move to the next lesson.		
6. I always tell my students up front what they must do to be successful, and for older students, I put it in writing in a rubric or matrix.		
7. I often use feedback in my classroom.		

WHAT DOES THE RESEARCH SAY?

In the government studies conducted by McREL (Marzano, 1998):

- When students learned to effectively identify similarities and differences between two or more topics, the effect size was 1.32 or 40 percentile points.
- When students were taught to create and effectively use advance organizers, the effect size was .48 or 18 percentile points.
- When students' note taking required them to generate personal linguistic representations of the information being presented, the effect size was .99 or 34 percentile points.
- When students used graphic representations (concrete models), the effect size was 1.24 or an increase in 39 percentile points.
- When students used some form of physical manipulation of concrete or symbolic artifacts, the effect size was .89 or 31 percentile points. Note that the use of computers as the vehicle for manipulatives produced the greatest gain: 43 percentile points.

6

Reflecting

Whenever students are being helped to see major concepts, big ideas, principles, and generalizations and not merely engaged in the pursuit of isolated facts, better teaching is going on. A fundamental goal of education is the ability to deal with various and competing ways of understanding the universe. Knowing how to spell is not enough.

—Martin Haberman (1997, p. 3)

Real-world connection could be called the "forgotten" part of the lesson. We talk to students about wars of the past, even have them memorize information about those wars, and often never talk to them about the wars that are imminent in their lifetime and strategies they need to know to avoid those wars. Dr. William Glasser (1994) said, "Our curriculum is worthless if we cannot convince students that they are learning useful life skills" (p. 1).

This part of the learning includes these two aspects:

1. Showing students how they are going to use the information in the real world. Example: After the completion of the unit on hunger in the United States, ask students to come up with possible solutions and evaluate those solutions based on feasibility in their world today. Use a matrix or mindmap to display the information.

2. Helping students reflect on the learning. This is a time of metacognition in which students evaluate the learning and its meaning to their world. Example: After a unit on immigration, ask students to graph the problems associated with too many people immigrating to one area. How does immigration affect the quality of life for the receiving country and for the countries

Figure 6.1   Strategic Learning Model: Reflecting

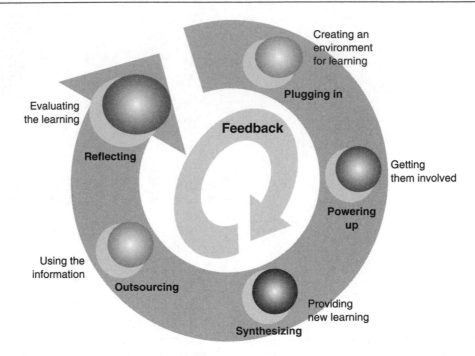

from which these people come? What are the solutions? What kinds of decisions will the students make in their lifetime that will affect immigration?

Another example: After a unit on slope, ask students to research the rules about slope for wheelchair access to public buildings. Do the buildings in the immediate area meet the standards?

The possibilities are endless. The key question that teachers must ask themselves as they develop units is, "What does this have to do with the life my students live now or will live in the future?" At last we are answering the age-old question students ask: "When are we ever going to use this information?" The answer is "now!"

Examples follow of four activities that can help bring the information you are teaching into the students' real world:

1. What, So What, Now What?

2. Ticket Out the Door

3. PMI (Plus, Minus, Interesting Observations)

4. Reflections

What, So What, Now What?

Students answer three questions about the lesson or unit after its completion.

The first question is, "What have I learned?" Students are asked to list key ideas that they learned from the lesson or unit.

The second question is, "So what difference does it make?" Students reflect on why they have learned the information.

The third question is, "Now what can I do with the learning?" Students reflect on what the new information has to do with their world. This is a guide for both students and teachers about the value of the lesson. The technique could also be used as an assessment of the learning or as a way to begin dialogue about real-world application.

Figure 6.2   "What, So What, Now What?"

What (have I learned)?
I have learned that world hunger is not caused by the lack of food produced but by a multitude of reasons, including transportation, politics, poverty, and a lack of infrastructure to ensure that farmers can survive.

So What (difference does it make)?
The problem will continue to grow without a workable plan. Because poverty and hunger often force people to harm the environment and others, the problem belongs to all of us.

Now What (can I do with this information)?
Awareness is the first step toward solving the problem. I must become more active in my own community to help solve the problems of hunger, and as a registered voter, I can make a difference by informed voting about issues that affect food production.

Ticket Out the Door

In this technique, students answer a question individually or in groups about the lesson. The answers are given to the teacher when the bell rings as the students' "ticket out the door." This technique is a great way for teachers to evaluate the effectiveness of the lesson because students who did not understand the lesson will not be able to give in-depth answers.

See Figure 6.3 for examples.

Figure 6.3   Ticket Out the Door

I Learned That
There are many reasons why people leave their countries to immigrate here. Some of the reasons are political, some are economic, some are social, and some are religious in nature.

I Changed my Mind About
The reasons people immigrate

Because
I looked at social, economic, political, and religious factors in the countries from which people leave to come to this country.

I Am Confused About
The discrepancies in immigration policies between states and countries

PMI (Plus, Minus, and Interesting Observations)

This is a technique originated by Edward DeBono (1985) in which students evaluate a lesson by listing the positive things they have learned in the Plus section, negative feelings in the Minus section, and interesting thoughts or ideas in the Interesting section. The purpose is to guide students to think about what they have learned.

See Figure 6.4 for some examples.

Figure 6.4   PMI (Plus, Minus, and Interesting Observations)

Directions: In the chart that follows, list something you have learned in this unit that will be helpful to you in the "Plus" section. List something you still don't understand or something you feel negative about in the "Minus" section. In the "Interesting" section, list something that you observed in the unit or an original idea that you have in regard to the learning.

Plus
The study of World War II demonstrated the power of people in the United States when they focused on the same objective.

Minus
I still believe the United States was slow getting involved.

Interesting
I think we should have a USO Day at our local nursing home and dress up in the clothes of the World War II era. We could provide entertainment music from that era. Many of those in nursing homes today Identify with that time—some even fought in the war.

Reflections

In this variation of Ticket Out the Door, students list three things they have learned and any unanswered questions. See Figure 6.5 for a sample list.

This is a good technique to do in the middle of a unit to determine whether students understand the information.

Figure 6.5   Three Major Learnings

Learned	Unanswered Questions
1. George Washington was born in Virginia and was a farmer.	Why did he refuse to run for a third term?
2. As the commander of the American army during the Revolutionary War, he is remembered for keeping up morale during the hard winter at Valley Forge.	How did the story of the cherry tree get started?
3. Some of the traits that he exhibited are courage, impartiality, and good judgment.	

Caprock Press (www.caprockpress.com) does a great job of helping students to reflect on the learning in their health materials. In one elementary example, students are given the following information about making good choices from school vending machines:

Many schools have made efforts to improve the snacks and beverages offered in their vending machines. In the past, vending machines offered foods with limited nutritional value such as sodas, candy, and a variety of high fat snacks, but healthy food items are becoming more common in today's schools. Vending companies are offering schools many options that include: Healthier drinks such as bottled water, 100% fruit juice and skim milk or healthier snacks such as nuts, dried fruits, trail mix, whole grain cereal bars, baked chips or crackers, pretzels and yogurt. (Caprock Press, 2005, n.p.)

Students are then asked to keep a snack log for one week and to evaluate their choices for snacks at school. Caprock takes the evaluation one step further by incorporating a real-world experience. They ask students to examine their school's policies on providing healthy choices for students.

SUMMARY

Reflections represents the part of the lesson in which students are given the opportunity to think about the learning, to examine it for deeper meaning, to relate it to their world and to self-evaluate.

Using Table 6.1, rate your comfort level with using reflections in your classroom.

Table 6.1   Rating Your Confidence Level for Reflecting

Rate your confidence in strategies to help your students reflect on the learning	Yes	No
1. I provide time for my students to reflect on what they have learned.		
2. I provide opportunities for my students to talk to one another about what they have learned.		
3. I provide opportunities for my students to question the learning or to clarify misunderstandings.		
4. I provide concrete models to help my students reflect.		
5. I provide feedback to my students that is both positive and prescriptive.		
6. I help my students to connect their learning to the real world.		

WHAT DOES THE RESEARCH SAY?

The effect size of this part of the learning model depends on the type and quality of feedback provided to the student. Feedback that is specific, diagnostic and prescriptive is the best kind in terms of increasing student achievement. Just saying, "good job" is not the kind of feedback that we mean here. The feedback must be very specific to the task and it should tell the student what he or she is doing right and then provide ways for improvement if needed.

Resource A

Sample Lesson Forms

BLANK SAMPLE LESSON FORM

Lesson _____

Title of Lesson:

Goals:

Classroom Management:

Groups:

Method:

Roles:

Materials:

The Learning Model

Plugging In: How will you ensure that the climate is conducive to learning?

1.

2.

3.

Powering Up: How will you ensure that students are involved in the learning?

1.

2.

3.

Synthesizing: How will you ensure that a variety of teaching tools are used so that all students are involved in the learning?

1.

2.

3.

Outsourcing: How will students use the information in meaningful ways?

1.

2.

3.

Reflecting: How will students make real-world connections to the learning?

1.

2.

3.

How will students evaluate their own learning?

1.

2.

3.

How will assessment be an ongoing part of the process?

Sample Lesson

Lesson _____

Title of Lesson: The Players at Yalta—World War II

Goals:
    To introduce the powers that influenced the Yalta Agreement: Stalin, Roosevelt, and Churchill

Classroom Management:
    Groups: 4 groups

Method: Students are given a ticket for a trip to Yalta as they enter the classroom. The tickets are color-coded:

    Purple—Stalin Group

    Green—Churchill Group

    Red—Roosevelt Group

    Yellow—News reporter

Roles: Leader, Spokesperson, Interpreter, and Timekeeper

Materials: Packets that include

    Background information

    Pieces of information about the person their group represents; each person has a different piece of information.

Rubric

KWL chart

Attribute Web

Find Someone Who

The Learning Model

Plugging In:
Mind Jog: Where Are You? (Clues about Yalta)
Techniques used: Think, Pair, Share; Pairs to Squares
Powering Up:
Fill out K of KWL chart, share answers with group and then with the class.
Next, fill out the W of the KWL chart and share information.

Synthesizing:

Each student becomes an expert on the piece of information they have been given in their packets.

Together in their groups they share attributes about the person they have been assigned.

Outsourcing:

Each group completes an attribute web about the person assigned.

Each group presents information to the class about the person assigned and answers questions about his role at Yalta and how that has affected us today.

Reflecting:

Find Someone Who (has information about World War II)

Self-Evaluation and Assessment:

Rubric on criteria for presentations

Resource B

Blackline Masters

ALIKE AND DIFFERENT

How Alike?		
How Different With Regard to		

APPOINTMENTS

Directions: Make appointments with 12 people in the room. Ask each student to initial the time of their appointment to work with you.

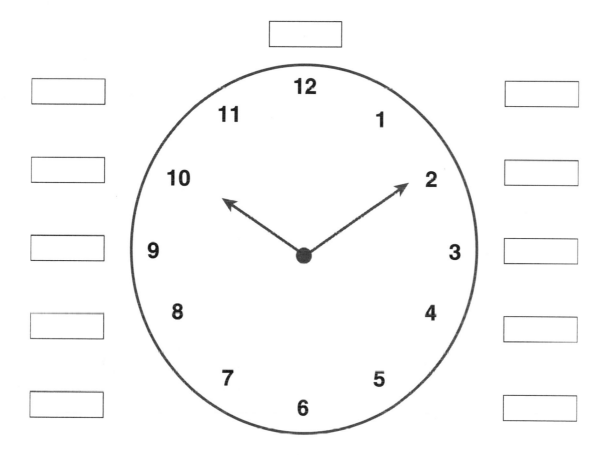

ATTRIBUTE WEB

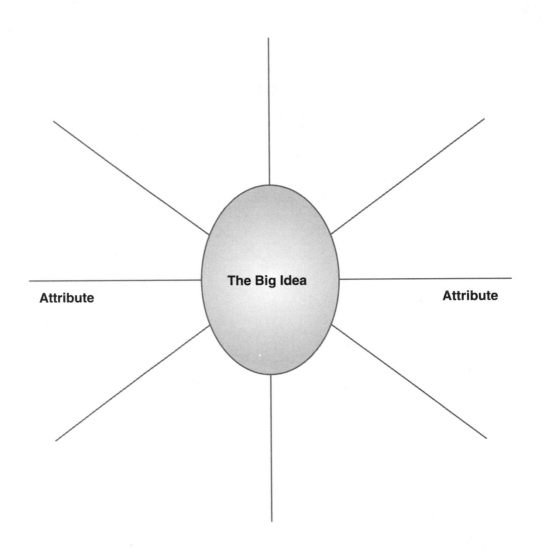

BEFORE AND AFTER

Directions: Before reading, place a T in the before-reading column if you believe the statement is true; place an F in the column if you believe the statement is false. After you have finished the unit, check to see if your answers were correct.

	Before Reading		Statement	After Reading	
	True	False		True	False
1.					
2.					
3.					
4.					
5.					

COLLABORATIVE RETELLING

First Retelling	Clued Retelling	Ideas

FAT AND SKINNY QUESTIONS

Directions: In the column for Fat questions, list questions that cannot be answered by "yes" or "no" or with one-word answers. Under the column for Skinny questions, list questions that can be answered with one-word answers.

	Fat?	Skinny?
1.		
2.		
3.		
4.		
5.		

FIND SOMEONE WHO

Directions: Ask a different person to sign for each of the following:

Find Someone Who	Sign Here	Person and Details
Likes the same sport as you		
Has a blue car		
Has two brothers		
Plans to go to college in another state		
Had an unusual summer job		
Plans to become a lawyer		
Likes to work with computers		
Has a birthday in December		
Has been to Disneyworld		
Has an unusual hobby		

FISHBONE

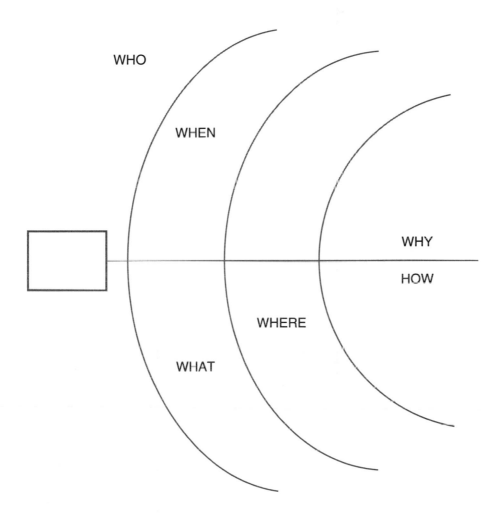

WHO

WHEN

WHY

HOW

WHERE

WHAT

KWL

Know	Want to Know	Learned

MINDMAP

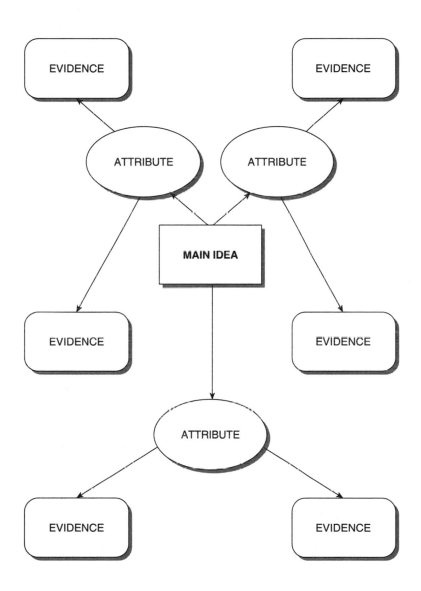

PMI (PLUS, MINUS, AND INTERESTING OBSERVATIONS)

Directions: In the chart that follows, list something you have learned in this unit that will be helpful to you in the "Plus" section. List something you still don't understand or something you feel negative about in the "Minus" section. In the "Interesting" section, list something that you observed in the unit or an original idea that you have in regard to the learning.

Plus

Minus

Interesting Observations

QUESTION-AND-ANSWER PROFILE

Directions: In your study groups, answer the questions that follow for each individual. Discuss areas where you are alike and areas where you are different as individuals.

Questions	First Person	Second Person	Third Person
My favorite musical group is			
My favorite sport is			
In my spare time I			
My best subject is			
If I could live anywhere, it would be			

THINKING AT RIGHT ANGLES

Directions: Fill in the mind map using concrete evidence from your text or other sources.

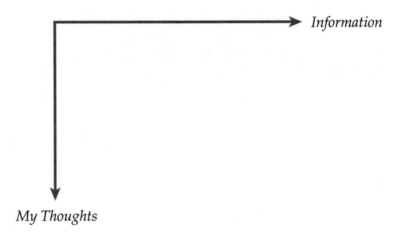

Information

My Thoughts

THREE MAJOR LEARNINGS

	I Learned	*Unanswered Questions*
1.		
2.		
3.		

TICKET OUT THE DOOR

I learned that

I changed my mind about

Because

I am confused about

VENN DIAGRAM: COMPARE AND CONTRAST

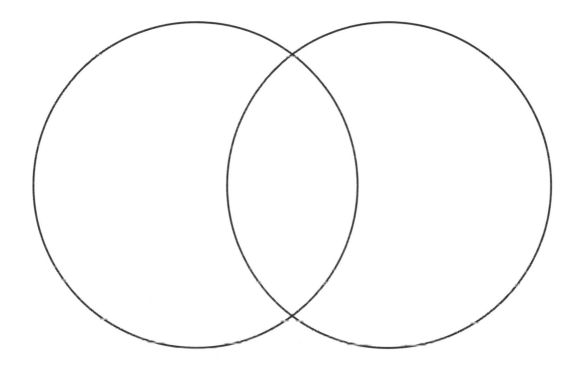

WHAT, SO WHAT, NOW WHAT

What (have I learned)?

So What (difference does it make)?

Now What (can I do with this information)?

References

Bellanca, J., & Fogarty, R. (1991). *Blueprints for thinking in the cooperative classroom*. Thousand Oaks, CA: Corwin Press.

Benton, J. (2005, October 31). Doesn't take a genius to see that China's catching up. *Dallas Morning News*, p. 21.

Caprock Press. (2005, October). *Healthy and wise*. Lubbock, TX: Author. Retrieved August 28, 2006, from http://www.caprockpress.com

DeBono, E. (1985). *Six thinking hats*. Toronto, Ontario, Canada: Key Porter.

Duffey, J., & Jonassen, D. (1992). *Constructivism and the technology of instruction: A conversation*. Hillsdale, NJ: Lawrence Erlbaum.

Friedman, T. L. (2005). *The world is flat*. NY: Farrar, Straus & Giroux

Glasser, W. (1994, March/April). Teach students what they will need in life. *ATPE News*, 20-21.

Glasser, W. (1997). A new look at school failure and school success. *Phi Delta Kappan, 78*(8), 599.

Golding, W., & Epstein, E. L. (1959). *Lord of the flies*. New York: Penguin Putnam.

Gough, P. B. (1988). The key to improving schools: An interview with William Glasser. *Phi Delta Kappan, 68*(9), 656.

Haberman, M. (1997). What star teaching actually looks like. *Instructional Leader, 10*(1), 3-5.

Hersey, J. (1985). *Hiroshima*. New York: Vintage.

Jensen, E. (1997). *Completing the puzzle: The brain-compatible approach to learning* (2nd ed.). Del Mar, CA: Turning Point.

Marzano, R.J. (1998). *A theory-based meta-analysis of research on instruction*. Aurora, CO: Mid-Continent Regional Educational Laboratory.

Marzano, R. J. (2001). *Designing a new taxonomy of educational objectives*. Thousand Oaks, CA: Corwin Press.

McCune, S. L.,Stephens, D. E., & Lowe, M. E. (1999). *Barron's how to prepare for the ExCET* (2nd ed.). Hauppaunge, NY: Barron's.

Pink, D. H. (2005). *A whole new mind: Moving from the information age to the conceptual age*. New York: Riverhead Books (a division of Penguin)

Scieszka, J., & Smith, L. (1995). *Math curse*. New York: Viking.

Sizer, T. (1992). *Horace's school: Redesigning the American high school*. Boston: Houghton Mifflin.

Tileston, D. W. (2004). *What every teacher should know about student motivation*. Thousand Oaks, CA: Corwin Press.

Tileston, D. W. (2006). *The silver bullet of high stakes testing*. Retrieved August 28, 2006, from http://www.whateveryteachershouldknow.com/donnaworkshops.html#bullet

Index